Hello, America!

Lincoln Memorial

by Kaitlyn Duling

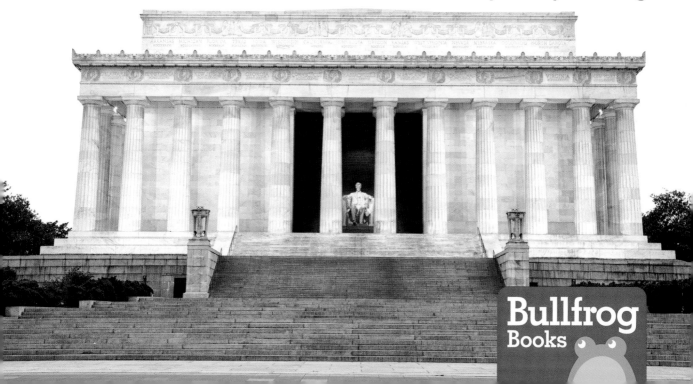

Bullfrog Books

Ideas for Parents and Teachers

Bullfrog Books let children practice reading informational text at the earliest reading levels. Repetition, familiar words, and photo labels support early readers.

Before Reading

Discuss the cover photo. What does it tell them?

Look at the picture glossary together. Read and discuss the words.

Read the Book

"Walk" through the book and look at the photos. Let the child ask questions. Point out the photo labels.

Read the book to the child, or have him or her read independently.

After Reading

Prompt the child to think more. Ask: What do you know about Abraham Lincoln? What more would you like to learn about him?

Bullfrog Books are published by Jump!
5357 Penn Avenue South
Minneapolis, MN 55419
www.jumplibrary.com

Library of Congress Cataloging-in-Publication Data

Names: Duling, Kaitlyn, author.
Title: Lincoln Memorial / by Kaitlyn Duling.
Description: Minneapolis, MN: Jump!, Inc., 2018.
Series: Hello, America! | Includes index.
Audience: Grade: K-3. | Audience: Age: 5-8.
Identifiers: LCCN 2017029252 (print)
LCCN 2017029864 (ebook)
ISBN 9781624966606 (e-book)
ISBN 9781620318683 (hard cover: alk. paper)
Subjects: LCSH: Lincoln Memorial (Washington, D.C.)—Juvenile literature.
Lincoln, Abraham, 1809-1865—Monuments
Washington (D.C.)—Juvenile literature.
Washington (D.C.)—Buildings, structures, etc.
Juvenile literature.
Classification: LCC F203.4.L73 D85 2017 (ebook)
LCC F203.4.L73 D85 2017 (print) | DDC 975.3—dc23
LC record available at https://lccn.loc.gov/2017029252

Editor: Kirsten Chang
Book Designer: Molly Ballanger
Photo Researcher: Molly Ballanger

Photo Credits: Gang Liu/Shutterstock, cover; Dan Thornberg/Shutterstock, 1; Curt Teich Postcard Archives/Alamy, 3; Jason Horowitz/Getty, 4; Orhan Cam/Shutterstock, 5, 23br, 23bl; ART Collection/Alamy, 6–7 (portrait); Hunter Bliss/Shutterstock, 6–7 (background); Everett Historical/Shutterstock, 8, 23tl; SuperStock/SuperStock, 9, 23ml; North Wind Picture Archives/Alamy, 10–11, 23tr; Circa Images/Alamy, 12–13; Stacy Gold/Getty, 14–15; Zack Frank/Shutterstock, 16, 22br; Mark Chivers/robertharding/Getty, 17; Michael Weber/Alamy, 18–19; Ronnachai Palas/Shutterstock, 20–21 (foreground); lazyllama/Shutterstock, 20–21 (background); M DOGAN/Shutterstock, 22tl; robert cicchetti/Shutterstock, 22bl; David Coleman/Alamy, 22tr; Praisaeng/Shutterstock, 23mr; mattesimages/Shutterstock, 24.

Printed in the United States of America at Corporate Graphics in North Mankato, Minnesota

Table of Contents

A Big Man

We are in Washington, D.C.

Look!

The Lincoln Memorial.

It is for Abraham Lincoln.
He was our 16th president.

It was during the Civil War.

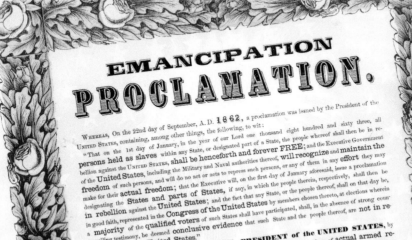

He signed a law.

It would end slavery.

He wanted to unite
the country.

He gave a
famous speech.

We remember him here.

When was it built?

1922.

We can go in.
We climb 87 steps.

His statue is inside.
What is it made of?
Marble.

marble

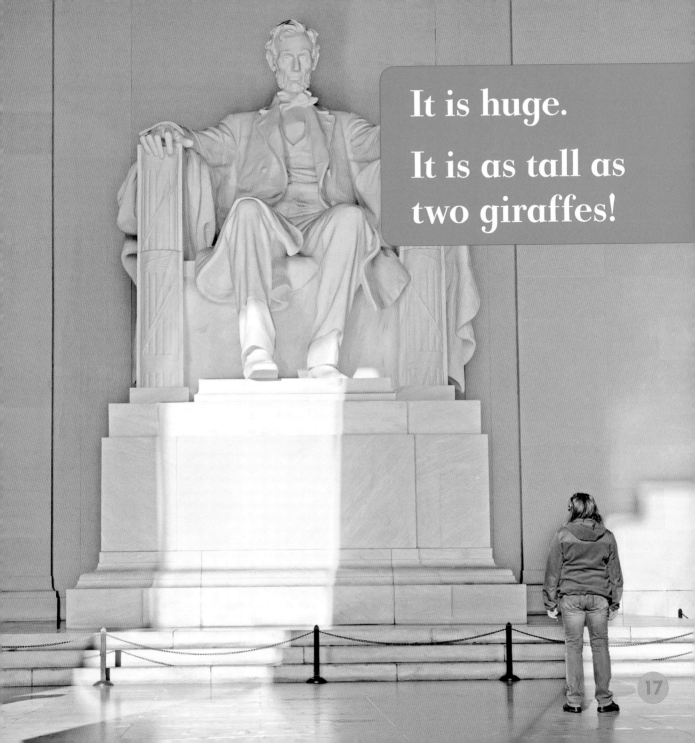

Here are his words.
We read them.

FELLOW COUNTRYMEN : AT THIS SE
APPEARING TO TAKE THE OATH OF THE
IDENTIAL OFFICE THERE IS LESS OCCA
FOR AN EXTENDED ADDRESS THAN
WAS AT THE FIRST · THEN A STATEM
SOMEWHAT IN DETAIL OF A COURSE T
PURSUED SEEMED FITTING AND PRO
NOW AT THE EXPIRATION OF FOUR YE
DURING WHICH PUBLIC DECLARATI
HAVE BEEN CONSTANTLY CALLED FO
ON EVERY POINT AND PHASE OF THE GR
CONTEST WHICH STILL ABSORBS THE
TENTION AND ENGROSSES THE ENERG
OF THE NATION LITTLE THAT IS N
COULD BE PRESENTED · THE PROGRESS
OUR ARMS UPON WHICH ALL ELSE CHIEF
DEPENDS IS AS WELL KNOWN TO THE PUBL
AS TO MYSELF AND IT IS I TRUST REASON
ABLY SATISFACTORY AND ENCOURAGING
ALL · WITH HIGH HOPE FOR THE FUTURE N
PREDICTION IN REGARD TO IT IS VENTUREL
ON THE OCCASION CORRESPONDING TC
THIS FOUR YEARS AGO ALL THOUGHTS WER
ANXIOUSLY DIRECTED TO AN IMPENDING
CIVIL WAR · ALL DREADED IT—ALL SOUGHT
TO AVERT IT · WHILE THE INAUGURAL AD-
DRESS WAS BEING DELIVERED FROM THIS
PLACE DEVOTED ALTOGETHER TO SAVING
THE UNION WITHOUT WAR INSURGENT
GENTS WERE IN THE CITY SEEKING TO DE-
ROY IT WITHOUT WAR—SEEKING TO DIS-
VE THE UNION AND DIVIDE EFFECTS BY
OTIATION · BOTH PARTIES DEPRECATED
BUT ONE OF THEM WOULD MAKE WAR
R THAN LET THE NATION SURVIVE

AND THE OTHER WOULD ACCEPT WAR RATHER THAN LET IT PERISH · AND THE WAR CAME · ONE EIGHTH OF THE WHOLE POPULATION WERE COLORED SLAVES NOT DISTRIBUTED GENERALLY OVER THE UNION BUT LOCALIZED IN THE SOUTHERN PART OF IT · THESE SLAVES CONSTITUTED A PECULIAR AND POWERFUL INTEREST · ALL KNEW THAT THIS INTEREST WAS SOMEHOW THE CAUSE OF THE WAR · TO STRENGTHEN PERPETUATE AND EXTEND THIS INTEREST WAS THE OBJECT FOR WHICH THE INSURGENTS WOULD REND THE UNION EVEN BY WAR WHILE THE GOVERNMENT CLAIMED NO RIGHT TO DO MORE THAN TO RESTRICT THE TERRITORIAL ENLARGEMENT OF IT · NEITHER PARTY EXPECTED FOR THE WAR THE MAGNITUDE OR THE DURATION WHICH IT HAS ALREADY ATTAINED · NEITHER ANTICIPATED THAT THE CAUSE OF THE CONFLICT MIGHT CEASE WITH OR EVEN BEFORE THE CONFLICT ITSELF SHOULD CEASE · EACH LOOKED FOR AN EASIER TRIUMPH AND A RESULT LESS FUNDAMENTAL AND ASTOUNDING · BOTH READ THE SAME BIBLE AND PRAY TO THE SAME GOD AND EACH INVOKES HIS AID AGAINST THE OTHER · IT MAY SEEM STRANGE THAT ANY MEN SHOULD DARE TO ASK A JUST GOD'S ASSISTANCE IN WRINGING THEIR BREAD FROM THE SWEAT OF OTHER MEN'S FACES BUT LET US JUDGE NOT THAT WE BE NOT JUDGED · THE PRAYERS OF BOTH COULD NOT BE ANSWERED ~ THAT OF NEITHER HAS BEEN ANSWERED FULLY · THE ALMIGHTY HAS HIS OWN PURPOSES · "WOE UNTO THE WORLD BECAUSE OF OFFENSES FOR IT MUST NEEDS BE THAT OFFENSES COME BUT WOE TO THAT MAN BY WHOM THE OFFENSE COMETH ·"

IF WE SHALL SUPPOSE THAT AMERICAN SLAVERY IS ONE OF THOSE OFFENSES WHICH IN THE PROVIDENCE OF GOD MUST NEEDS COME BUT WHICH HAVING CONTINUED THROUGH HIS APPOINTED TIME HE NOW WILLS TO REMOVE AND THAT HE GIVES TO BOTH NORTH AND SOUTH THIS TERRIBLE WAR AS THE WOE DUE TO THOSE BY WHOM THE OFFENSE CAME SHALL WE DISCERN THEREIN ANY DEPARTURE FROM THOSE DIVINE ATTRIBUTES WHICH THE BELIEVERS IN A LIVING GOD ALWAYS ASCRIBE TO HIM · FONDLY DO WE HOPE ~ FERVENTLY DO WE PRAY ~ THAT THIS MIGHTY SCOURGE OF WAR MAY SPEEDILY PASS AWAY · YET IF GOD WILLS THAT IT CONTINUE UNTIL ALL THE WEALTH PILED BY THE BONDSMAN'S TWO HUNDRED AND FIFTY YEARS OF UNREQUITED TOIL SHALL BE SUNK AND UNTIL EVERY DROP OF BLOOD DRAWN WITH THE LASH SHALL BE PAID BY ANOTHER DRAWN WITH THE SWORD AS WAS SAID THREE THOUSAND YEARS AGO SO STILL IT MUST BE SAID "THE JUDGMENTS OF THE LORD ARE TRUE AND RIGHTEOUS ALTOGETHER ·"

WITH MALICE TOWARD NONE WITH CHARITY FOR ALL WITH FIRMNESS IN THE RIGHT AS GOD GIVES US TO SEE THE RIGHT LET US STRIVE ON TO FINISH THE WORK WE ARE IN TO BIND UP THE NATION'S WOUNDS TO CARE FOR HIM WHO SHALL HAVE BORNE THE BATTLE AND FOR HIS WIDOW AND HIS ORPHAN TO DO ALL WHICH MAY ACHIEVE AND CHERISH A JUST AND LASTING PEACE AMONG OURSELVES AND WITH ALL NATIONS ·

Thank you, Lincoln!

Parts of the Memorial

columns
The memorial has 36 marble columns, one for each state when Lincoln was president.

murals
Two murals are painted above the speeches. They represent Lincoln's life.

marble statue
Lincoln's statue is made of marble. Marble is a hard, polished stone with streaks of color.

speeches
Two of Lincoln's speeches are on the walls. They are the Gettysburg Address and Second Inaugural Address.

Picture Glossary

Civil War
A U.S. war in which two groups of people from the United States fought each other.

slavery
The practice of forcing people to work as slaves.

law
A rule that people must follow.

unite
To come together as one.

memorial
A place meant to help remember a person or event.

Washington, D.C.
The capital of the United States.

Index

To Learn More

Learning more is as easy as 1, 2, 3.

1) Go to www.factsurfer.com

2) Enter "LincolnMemorial" into the search box.

3) Click the "Surf" button to see a list of websites.

With factsurfer.com, finding more information is just a click away.